CRYPTOCURRENCY
FOMO

How to get into Bitcoin without really caring what Bitcoin is.

The information provided in this book is an opinion and is for information purposes only. It is not intended to be investment advice. Investing involves risk. Seek a duly licensed professional for investment advice.

Table of Contents:

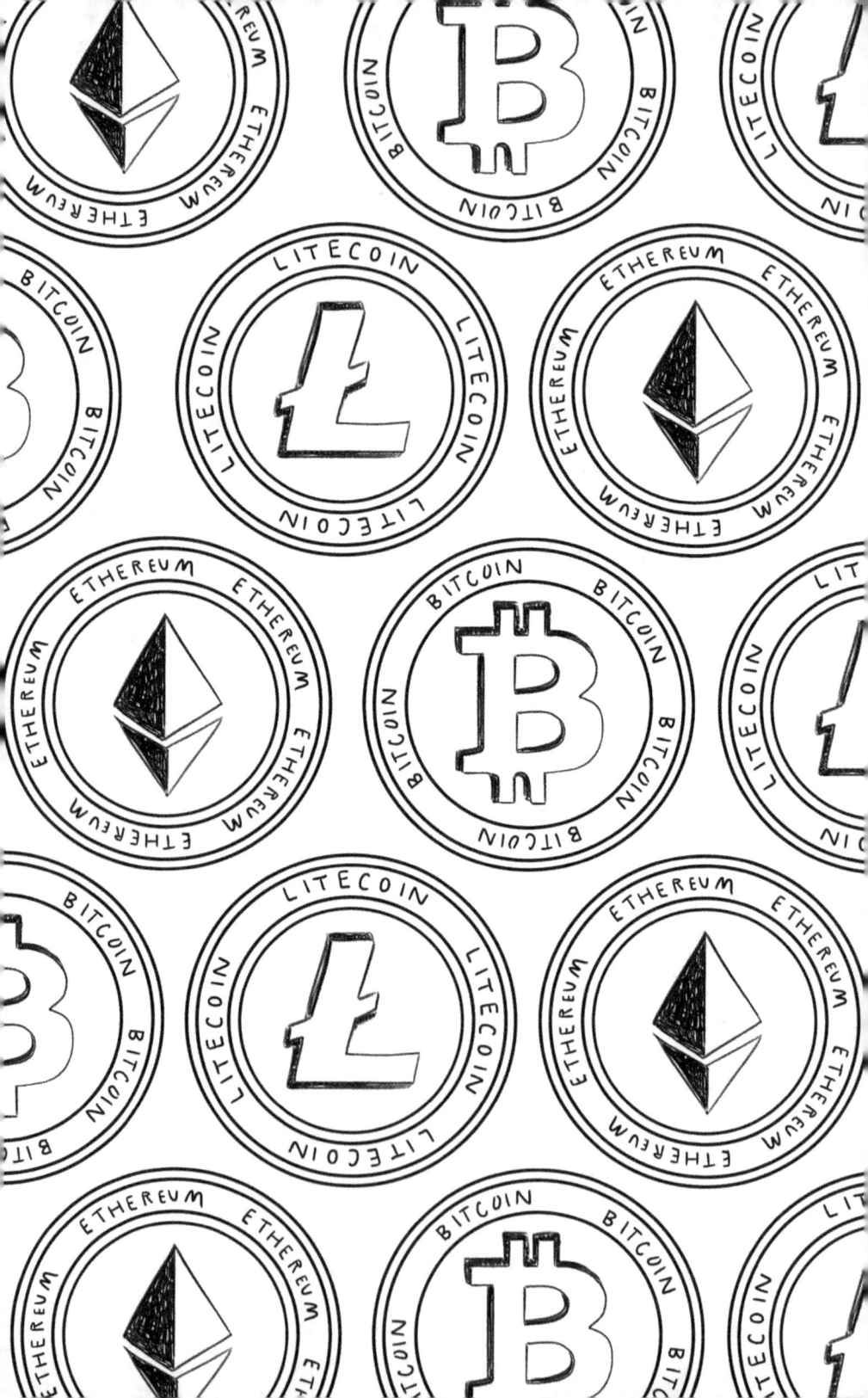

Introduction

The creation and adoption of Bitcoin and the Blockchain technologies will become one of the largest technological disruptions that we will see in our lifetimes. From, Banks to Credit Scores to Hospitals to Car Manufacturers, virtually any industry that you can think of will feel the impact of this revolutionary technology. We are beginning to witness the greatest transfer of wealth that we will ever see.

Even though it may seem like everyone is talking about Bitcoin and Cryptocurrencies, the simple fact that you are reading this book makes you one of the early adopters.

Educate yourselves, begin investing, and strap in for a very wild and exciting ride!

"Markets are constantly in a state of uncertainty and flux and money is made by discounting the obvious and betting on the unexpected."

-George Soros

Money, Markets, Made

CHAPTER 1

Introducing Bitcoin

What is Bitcoin?

This is something that every potential investor asks before taking the dive. However, it's also the question least answered. I don't mean that people don't try to answer, but their answer is usually drawn out and leaves their inquisitor more confused. It's a difficult answer to give, but to the unfortunate luck of the asker, most give it wrong. As difficult as it may be, I will attempt to explain it as succinctly and all-encompassing as possible. Well......here goes nothing.

Bitcoin is a Cryptocurrency

It can be sent, received, and earned (through mining) from one user to another anywhere in the world. Each Bitcoin functions on a massive public ledger, also known as a blockchain. This ledger contains the information from each confirmed transaction on the blockcahin. Once a transaction is confirmed it will then become a 'block' within the blockchain, or, in other words, an entry onto the public ledger.

Transactions are maintained (confirmed) through Peer to Peer technology. This technology is a network of computers around the globe that all communicate, agree, and verify each transaction.

Bitcoin is Decentralized

Now here's where things get real interesting. Bitcoin's supply, and the supply of any cryptocurrency with a decentralized blockchain, cannot be controlled by a single entity. It is entirely decentralized, unable to be manipulated by any one government, bank, corporation, or central server. This in turn means that anyone who owns Bitcoin has full control of those coins at all times.

Bitcoin is a Blockchain

Its underlying value is entirely dependent upon whether or not people use, or don't use, its blockchain technology. Whether you're a Bitcoin skeptic or enthusiast, it's hard to deny the immense potential and incredible ingenuity of the blockchain technology.

What to Know About Bitcoin

DYOR

Before I dive into the ins and outs of Bitcoin and Digital Assets, I want to stress the importance of Do Your Own Research. Always begin any investment endeavor researching how it works and more importantly how it best works for you. Investing in anything is never as straight forward as it seems so always begin by doing your due diligence. The fact that you're reading this book is a great start. It shows that you're willing to take the time to learn before diving in. However, you should still treat this book as a jumping- off-point. Trading digital assets is a vast topic with roots in many of the financial markets we are all familiar with today. Textbooks upon textbooks could be filled on this subject, so please use this book as a means to discover where further research is needed based on the crypto investments that are right for you.

Know Your Limitations

There are usually weekly limits to how much you can buy or cash out cryptocurrencies with fiat currency such as USD. These limits are based on the volume of trading you do, account verification, and the length of time that your account has been opened for. If you view this as an issue, do not fret as this is only a brief setback as your account limit will increase after a few weeks or months depending on those factors.

Beware the Fees

Nothing in life is free and this includes buying Bitcoin and other cryptocurrencies. Whether buying, selling, or sending cryptocurrency, there will be a fee that comes along with it. They can be high if your cryptocurrency is volatile and expensive, but they do get cheaper as the amounts you purchase get larger.

Double the Authenticity

When setting up your different accounts in the crypto stratosphere you will see an option in the account security section of each website or app called 2-Factor Authentication or 2FA. ALWAYS SET THIS UP! It is additional security for your online account, and is strictly there to better secure your digital assets. Later in the book I will expand on this extra layer of security, but in the beginning you need to recognize that 2FA is an important aspect to the security of your cryptocurrencies.

You don't have to buy a whole coin!

A common misconception when it comes to purchasing Bitcoin and other cryptocurrencies is that you have to buy the whole coin. This couldn't be farther from the truth. In reality you can buy small fractions at a time. How small? To be precise, Bitcoin is divisible up to eight decimal places. This means, in theory, you could own 0.00000001BTC. Compare this to the US $ being limited to two decimal places, and all this means Bitcoin is a more perfect unit of account than the dollar.

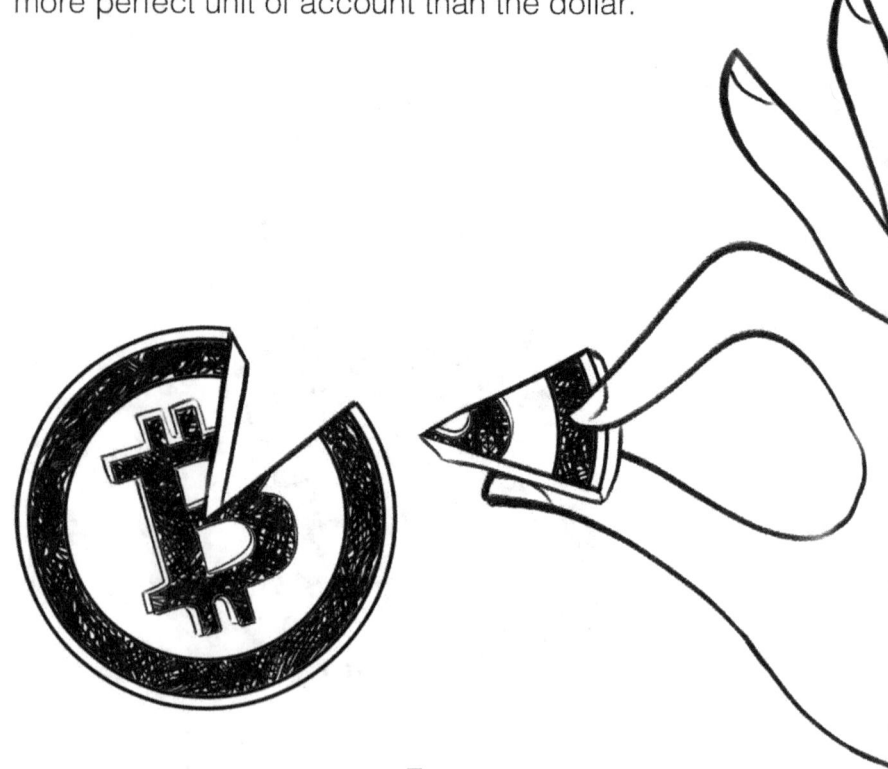

What goes up must come down

By now everyone's heard a story about average Joe going from IT clerk to crypto-millionaire over these past years. While this is exciting do not let this fool you into thinking it will always go up. Huge gains mean huge losses. With every big surge in price a massive drop in value will follow. Whatever you do don't panic and let your emotions get the best of you. Keep cool, be calm, and hold on. I'll reiterate DYOR: Do thorough research beforehand and buy the right coins. This way when those days come, you'll have nothing to worry about. In fact days of red will become a god send because it's a fire sale and all your favorite coins are half off. There will be plenty of big ups but always keep in mind that what goes up must come down.

Buy The Dips!

Buy low, sell high. As cliché as it might sound, this one mindset could generate scours of profit for you. As long as you never invest 100% of your cash immediately and always have some spare capital on the sidelines waiting for the right opportunity, then when there is a large correction in the markets and people are panicking, do not sell, this is the time to buy more while all of your favorite coins are on sale.

Vegas Rules Apply

NEVER RISK MORE THAN YOU CAN AFFORD TO LOSE. I know it's another cliché, but this proverbial truth should always be on your mind when you begin testing your luck in the crypto market. Nothing is guaranteed! If you are seeing massive gains from your crypto investments, it may be a good time to de-risk by pulling out some or all of your initial investment.

CHAPTER 2

Setting Up Your Account
&
Buying Bitcoin

11

How to Buy Bitcoin

This section will be mainly concerned with how you can turn your fiat money, such as US Dollars, into Bitcoin. Currently, Coinbase is one of the most popular and user friendly exchanges to complete this feat. Coinbase makes it easy to buy Bitcoin, along with a few other coins, using your bank account, credit (for the mean time), and debit card. At the time this book is being written purchasing Bitcoin on credit is coming under increasing scrutiny so be sure to check Coinbase's accepted payments under the FAQ section on their website for the most up-to-date and accurate information regarding types of payment methods accepted.

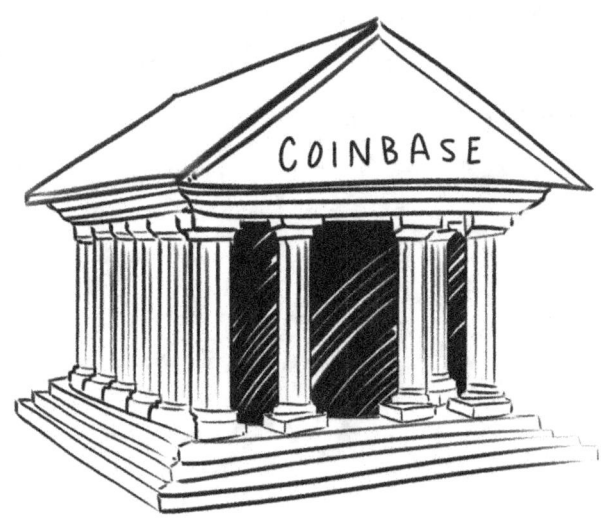

Also, at the time of writing this book, the stock investing app called RobinHood is rumored to begin trading cryptocurrencies with no fees. Once this is announced, it may be worth looking into for smaller beginner accounts looking to minimize fees.

Although I'm using Coinbase to establish a common example so that the steps I'm about to outline are easier to connect to, it does not mean that these steps are only for Coinbase. The process that I will walk you through for Coinbase is very similar to the process you will follow for any other exchange sites when purchasing crypto with your country's currency. Coinbase is also one of the more forgiving exchanges and serves as a perfect platform for the beginner crypto-investor.

Setting Up Your Account

Some Things You Will Need:

- Coinbase.com

- Email

- Bank or Credit Card Account information

- Access to your Bank or Credit Cards' website

- Form of Photo ID: (US Customers Must use a

Government-Issued Photo ID)

- Camera Phone or Working Webcam (For Verification, I'll

explain later)

Step 1

Go to Coinbase.com and click Sign Up in the top right side of the screen.

Provide:

1. Your name
2. Email address
3. Create a strong password
4. Select your state of residency (US Citizens)
5. Carefully review the terms of the User Agreement and Privacy Policy

After you've reviewed to your satisfaction, click **Create Account**

Step 2

Verifying Email and Phone

You should now find yourself on a page saying to check your email. Navigate to your email's inbox. Once there, find the Coinbase email and select the Verify Your Email box. When you click on that you will be asked to provide your phone number. Enter your mobile phone number and make sure it's close by. Shortly thereafter you'll receive a text message containing a 7-digit number. After you are brought to the final page enter this number in the required field.

Word to the Wise: This is time sensitive code. Do not wait; enter this code in immediately in order to ensure you are verified quickly.

Step 3

Verifying Your Account

For most people this next step can be alarming, but I promise you it is nothing to worry about. This is for tax purposes and ultimately your safety. Not only does it add an extra layer of security but it's very quick and easy. If you are a US customer and already have an electronically scanned copy of your ID then you can skip a step and head to Upload below. All others should continue on if you wish to do this properly. US customers must have a US state-issued ID such as a driver's license and may either scan or snap a photo with their phone or webcam, for account verification upload. All others located outside of the US must use the mobile camera or webcam option, as of January 2018. You can choose to upload the photos via your computer's webcam, mobile camera, or file scanner.

(For tips on taking and completing this photo please visit the address below:

https://support.coinbase.com/customer/en/portal/articles/1220621-id entity-verification)

If you choose to upload with your mobile phone, a link will be sent to the phone number provided in the previous

Step 4

Cash or Credit

In the Coinbase Home Page, scroll down and find the Complete your account header on the left-hand side. Click on Select your payment method and enter in your preferred payment method. Setting up your pay method can also be done by selecting Settings. When brought to the settings page you will see six options now displayed underneath the same options from the Home Page. You'll need Linked Accounts for setting up a payment method. Select this and then select the blue Link Account

Step 5

The Finish Line

Open up your bank or credit card's website and go to your account's recent transactions. Look for two charges between one and two dollars from Coinbase. Do not fret, these transactions are only temporary. Jot down the cents part of the transaction, eg .15 if $1.15 or .31 if $1.31, and click back to Coinbase's website. Enter these two transactions in the boxes provided and....

CONGRATULATIONS!!!!!

You're verified and ready to buy you're first digital currency.

Word to the Wise: After you've verified your payment account Coinbase may ask you if you'd like to purchase a small $ amount of Bitcoin. I suggest you wait and purchase all of your digital currency at once because remember there are extra fees between crypto and physical currency and these fees are sometimes more expensive with smaller transactions.

Filling Up Your Digital Wallet with Digital Currency

Coinbase offers a few coins for which you can purchase with your bank account, debit or credit card. I suggest you do your research and understand the different pros and cons of each coin in order to find the coin(s) which better suites your desired use in the crypto-stratosphere. We will not go into purchasing each type as it is virtually identical for all. So, for the sake of simplicity, we're going to use Bitcoin to illustrate our steps below.

Back on Coinbase's Home Page you will want to find the Buy/Sell with this symbol next to it (below). Because we're buying our first digital currencies you will want to make sure you are in the Buy tab on this page and not the Sell tab.

Step 1
Find and select your digital currency. In this example we've chosen Bitcoin.

Step 2
Choose your desired payment method using the drop-down menu.

Step 3
Enter the desired amount in $ or BTC.

Step 4
Click "Buy Bitcoin Instantly"

You now own Bitcoin!

When you go to view your digital wallet your digital currency purchased will be reflected as a positive balance in this wallet and you'll be able to view how much you're holdings are worth in your home currency.

Lock Down Your Account with an Extra Layer of Security:

2FA (Two Factor Authentication) is an extra level of security that you can choose to set up. It works by utilizing a secret code that is shared by your exchange and an app on your cellphone. This secret code allows the app to generate a secret 6 digit access code that changes every 30 seconds. This ensures that your accounts cannot be accessed unless your personal cellphone is also present to supply you with the access code.

2FA doesn't have to be setup immediately, but it is simple and is something that should be done as soon as possible.

Step 1

To setup 2FA for any exchange, simply navigate to the security tab of your exchange and select Two-Factor Authentication.

Step 2

On your smart phone, go to the App Store and download the "Google Authenticator" app.

Step 3

Your exchange will provide you with a Secret Key. Write this down somewhere safe for backup purposes and then enter or scan it into your "Google Authenticator" App.

That's it! Now when you log into your exchange or attempt to send your coins somewhere, the exchange will verify that it is you by requesting the 6-digit code provided by your app.

CHAPTER 3

So I Bought Bitcoin...
Now What?

Now that you're a proud Bitcoin owner, you will want to utilize this digital asset in a way that best fits your financial needs and ambitions as well as your lifestyle. In this chapter I will provide you with an overview of the main two options that precede your purchase of Bitcoin. This way you can make an informed decision about which is the right next step for you. After entering the crypto arena, you will want to identify the method which best fits your investment goals and strategies.

Considering The Options

OPTION #1

Become a Crypto-Trader

If you have a high risk tolerance, possess a significant amount of experience or genuinely enjoy buying and selling stocks, then this first option may be for you. However, if you do go this route I encourage you to be prepared to invest hours of your time reading up on news and researching trends. This option will involve you using your Bitcoin to buy and sell other Digital Assets and Tokens called Altcoins. In the next chapter, I will layout a brief summary of what you will need to help navigate yourself through the vast ocean of crypto-exchanges

OPTION #2

HODL (Hold)

If Option #1 seems too complicated, time-consuming, or just simply not what you're aiming to do in the crypto-world, then you should consider a more passive strategy. This would involve you storing your digital assets somewhere safe, similar to a savings account, and either waiting for the coin to appreciate or earning a return from where your coins are being held. This shifts your main concern from trends to security. In Chapter 5, I will lay out some options for storing your digital assets so you can buy them and forget about them. HODL (Holding On for Dear Life) as the market swings back and forth from jubilation to condemnation.

CHAPTER 4

How To Trade Cryptocurrencies

Trading Bitcoins for Altcoins

At this point, you have created an account with Coinbase and have purchased some Bitcoin. You are now invested in cryptocurrency. However there are hundreds of other cryptocurrencies (often called Altcoins) that you can invest in other than the few you can currently purchase on Coinbase.

Cryptocurrency Online Exchanges

If you're familiar with the stock market then you may skip ahead as these exchanges operate in an almost identical fashion. If you're not familiar with stock trading, then it's best to think of exchanges as an online market, similar to Ebay, where you can exchange your Bitcoin, Ethereum, Litecoin, etc. for other cryptocurrencies. And, much like Ebay, the price you pay depends on how many people are buying or selling that coin and the price driving the demand to buy and sell. However, unlike Ebay, the price you pay is in Bitcoin, not USD, GBP, EUR, AUD, CD, etc. It's because of this that you want to switch your thinking when buying from your home currency to Bitcoin.

What is an Altcoin?

An Altcoin is term used for any digital cryptocurrency other than Bitcoin. It is said to stand for "Alternative to Bitcoin". An Altcoin could differ from Bitcoin in a variety of different ways.

Some are created to transfer faster and with less fees, others have a different economic model, or focus on privacy, while some are even created specifically to interact one day with all connected household appliances.

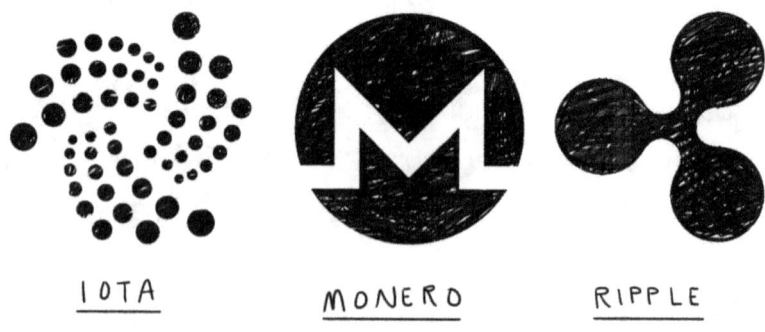

IOTA   MONERO   RIPPLE

Before selecting an Altcoin to invest in, it is important that you do your due diligence because although some Altcoins may see price increases well over 1,000% or even 10,000%, many Altcoins may turn out to be projects with a poor development teams or projects that aren't even close to any sort of usable product. Some Altcoins can even be flat out scams, although this will become less and less common as regulation increases. It is important that you do your own research. At the end of this book, I will provide links to get you started.

How to Buy Altcoins

The steps to purchase any Altcoin is simple.

Step 1

Sign up to Coinbase and purchase Bitcoin (Completed)

Step 2

Sign up to an Altcoin Exchange that lists the Altcoin of your choice.

Step 3

Send your Bitcoin from Coinbase Account to an Online Exchange Account that you just created.

Step 4

Now your new Altcoin Exchange contains your Bitcoin and you're all set to go and spend that Bitcoin to buy some shiny new Altcoins!

Word to the Wise: When researching a particular Altcoin, Coinmarketcap.com can act as a valuable tool to find out which exchanges list the coin you want to invest in. It will also tell you which exchanges you can use to purchase the coin that you are researching

Buying Altcoins

There is no shortage of online exchanges. Always DYOR before sending your coins to any online exchange.

Determine which exchange is right for you.

Exchanges are not created equal, all differing when it comes to:

• Which coins and tokens you can buy
• Level of security provided
• Transaction fees charged
• Credibility.

DYOR and determine which exchange is right for you!

Step 1: Sign up to Coinbase (Completed in Chapter 2)

Step 2: Registering with an Online Exchange

You will first need to register for an online exchange (see the end of Chapter 4 for a list of exchanges)

After you have done a thorough job researching each exchange you will need to register on their website and create an account. Because the steps to sign up are much the same as those for signing up for Coinbase, I'm not going to spell out each step. Instead, I will dive straight into what we have not covered, how to send and receive your coins from exchanges using your digital wallet addresses.

Step 3: Sending/Transferring Coins

How to Withdraw & Deposit Bitcoin

Step 3.1: Find Your Wallets

Starting from the homepage of your online exchange's homepage, find and click on Wallets, Funds, or Deposits/Withdrawals tab. This page is where you'll be able to track the growth of your account balance after you've become an active trader.

Step 3.2: Find Your Bitcoin Wallet

Once in your exchange's wallet page, locate Bitcoin
(BTC) in the list of coins under your Account Balances.
Once you've located it, you'll see a selection for "+" and
"-", or labeled Deposits and Withdraw. Because you will
be receiving Bitcoin from your Coinbase account you'll
want to select the "Deposit" or "+" option. When you click
on this option it should reveal your BTC wallet address
which is where you will send your Bitcoin deposits. Copy
this address and be very careful you copy ONLY your
wallet address and nothing else. If this address is
incorrect in any way your Bitcoin will never make it to your
wallet. Now it's time to navigate back to Coinbase.

Step 3.3: Send Bitcoin to Your Bitcoin Wallet

In Coinbase, go to the Accounts tab and click Send (Arrow Symbol) under your BTC Wallet. Paste the Bitcoin wallet address that you copied in the previous step. (**DOUBLE CHECK THAT IT'S CORRECT!**) Enter the amount you wish to send, hit Max if you want to send your entire balance, and your Bitcoin should be available in your chosen online exchange shortly.

Step 3.4: Wait.......

Do not be alarmed that your Bitcoin did not immediately arrive. Bitcoin, while popular and well known, is one of the slowest coins and the speed with which it transfers depends on your exchange's transaction volume and how many miners are operating. No matter your exchange, it should show any Pending Deposits, locate this area and watch there for eta of your Bitcoin.

Step 4: Buy Altcoins

Once your Bitcoin arrives in your account and is no longer showing as Pending, you can go to the "Markets" or "Exchange" tab and purchase any Altcoin listed on that exchange. The process is even easier than transferring Bitcoin. Simply:

1. Find your coin under the Bitcoin Markets
2. Find the Buy and Sell section or tabs
3. Enter the Quantity of coins you wish to purchase
4. Set your price as the Bid, Ask, or Market price*
5. Click place order

*Note: the purchase price is in Bitcoin, not US Dollars
It's as easy as that!

Below are the top 15 exchanges in terms of US $ volume and value. I've provided you with this table to help get your search started. There are literally hundreds of exchanges out there that you will have the option to choose from.

#	Exchange	Pair	Volume (24h)	BTC Price ($)
1	OKEx	BTC/USDT	$1,221,580,000	$8,289.49
2	Bitfinex	BTC/USD	$1,091,470,000	$8,289.00
3	Binance	BTC/USDT	$563,321,000	$8,319.06
4	GDAX	BTC/USD	$558,937,000	$8,319.98
5	bitFlyer	BTC/JPY	$414,265,000	$8,358.37
6	Bitstamp	BTC/USD	$386,179,000	$8,310.56
7	Upbit	BTC/KRW	$322,181,000	$8,254.54
8	Kraken	BTC/EUR	$294,674,000	$8,329.48
9	Huobi	BTC/USDT	$228,980,000	$8,266.16
10	Gemini	BTC/USD	$158,416,000	$8,336.89
11	Bithumb	BTC/KRW	$150,424,000	$8,255.46
12	Poloniex	BTC/USDT	$126,611,000	$8,343.44
13	Bittrex	BTC/USDT	$101,673,000	$8,295.41
14	Bitinka	BTC/EUR	$84,480,100	$8,285.86
15	HitBTC	BTC/USDT	$68,885,100	$8,380.50

*data provided by Coinbase.com 2/7/2018

CHAPTER 5

HODL: Ways To Hold and Secure Your Bitcoin

Crypto Wallets

A Cryptocurrency Wallet is a digital software that is used to send, receive, and store your cryptocurrencies. It can be a desktop program, a physical printout, or even a physical offline drive similar to a thumb drive. Whether you are holding the coins in an online exchange, in a desktop wallet that you downloaded or in a physical offline wallet, cryptocurrencies are always stored on some type of wallet.

Types of Wallets

Desktop Wallets:

Desktop wallets are one of the most popular and secure ways to store your coins. These wallets are available through download and run on your computer. The wallet can be only accessed from that one computer. The primary risk with a Desktop Wallet is that your computer is hacked or gets a virus.

Examples:

-Electrum

-HolyTransaction

-MultiBit

-Armory

Word to the Wise: A coin will usually recommend a few wallets that it is known to be compatible with

Mobile Wallets:

A wallet that is ran from an app on your smartphone.

Online Wallets:

Online wallets can be accessed from anywhere by any device because they run on the cloud. Online wallets are very convenient; however, your private keys are held by a third party and are kept online which makes them more vulnerable to hackers. An example of an online wallet is the wallet you use on each exchange such as Binance or Bittrex.

Hardware Wallet:

A hardware wallet is a physical device that allows you store your cryptocurrencies offline and away from hackers. One of the most common hardware wallets is the Ledger Nano S which is a USB type device. Only purchase directly from the manufacturer and make sure that you write down the 24 word recovery phrase that the device provides to you when you set it up and keep those 24 words very very safe. The recovery phrase is what retrieves your coins if your hardware wallet is lost or damaged.

Examples:

-Ledger Nano S
-Trezor

Paper Wallet:

A paper wallet is very simple to use and quick to setup. A paper wallet is a physical offline printout of your public and private keys that you must keep in a very safe location. A paper wallet can be created using WalletGenerator.net. Once you create the paper wallet on one of those sites, you simply print out your public and private keys and then you can send your coins from any exchange to your public wallet key printed on your piece of paper. This is one of the safest methods to store your cryptocurrency coins.

Examples:

-WalletGenerator.net
-Myetherwallet.com

Setting up a Paper Wallet

Step 1
Visit the page WalletGenerator.net.

Step 2
Download the zip file shown in "Step 0" on the site.

Step 3
Once downloaded, before you go any further, disconnect your computer from the internet to ensure that this whole process is hidden from potential hackers. Now proceed to open the "index.html" file.

Step 4
Now we will generate your wallet. Keep hovering over the highlighted text or manually type in random characters in the box to make your private key even more random.
Just keep doing it until the counter goes to "0". Then your wallet will be generated.

Step 5
Print the page or make more than one copy of the public and private keys that are shown. Store your private keys VERY safely.

Conclusion

Cryptocurrencies and the blockchain will be the way of the future. They will massively disrupt almost any industry that you can think of and they will completely reshape the way that many things are currently done today.

As with any major new innovation, there will be ups and downs, surges and crashes, fans and critics, and a slow but steady cycle of adoption.

This will be one of the largest transfers of wealth that we will ever see, but like anything else, this will take time.

In the meantime, the best thing to do is to invest something so that you have some skin in the game, have patience, and never stop educating yourself.

I wish you nothing but prosperity on this exciting journey that we are now on together!

Helpful Sites, Apps, and Podcasts

WEBSITES	APPS	PODCASTS
Coinmarketcap	Blockfolio	Chat w/ Traders
MyCryptoTools	Tab Trader	Crypto 101
BitcoinTalk	Coinmarket App	The Bad Crypto
CoinTelegraph	Drakdoo	Unchained
BitcoinWisdom	Delta	Coin Mastery
CoinDesk	Coin Market Cap	
CoinHills		
Reddit		
CryptoCompare		
TradingView		
Coinigy